Explore the Inca Trail

**Jacquetta Megarry
and Roy Davies**

Rucksack Readers

Explore the Inca Trail: a Rucksack Reader

First edition published 2002 by Rucksack Readers, Landrick Lodge, Dunblane, FK15 0HY, UK

Telephone 01786 824 696 (+44 1786 824 696)

Fax   01786 825 090 (+44 1786 825 090)

Website   **www.rucsacs.com**

Email   **info@rucsacs.com**

Distributed in North America by Interlink Publishing, 46 Crosby Street, Northampton, Mass., 01060, USA (www.interlinkbooks.com)

Distributed in Peru by Libreria SBS, Av. El Sol, 781-A, Cusco, Peru (cusco@sbs.com.pe)

ISBN 1-898481-12-1

British Library cataloguing in publication data: a catalogue record for this book is available from the British Library.

Designed by Workhorse Productions (info@workhorse.co.uk)
Reprographics by Digital Imaging, printing by M&M Press Ltd, Glasgow
The maps in this book were created by Cartographic Consultants of Edinburgh © 2001/02

Publisher's note
Walking on narrow, steep paths at altitude involves possible health hazards. These are explained as clearly as possible, and advice offered on how to minimise them. All information has been checked carefully prior to publication. However, individuals are responsible for their own welfare and safety, and the publisher cannot accept responsibility for any ill-health or injury, however caused.

Explore the Inca Trail: contents

Introduction

The Inca Trail to Machu Picchu* is unlike any other hike. You may be able to walk up mountains that are higher or tougher, to visit archaeological sites that are older or larger, or to find nature reserves with more or rarer species. But there is nowhere on earth where you will experience such a gratifying combination of stunning scenery, physical challenge and spectacular plant life. And hiking the trail is only an extended prelude to arriving at arguably the most photogenic ruins on the planet.

Machu Picchu combines mystery, beauty and history in equal proportions. It represents the apogee of an ancient civilisation that was destroyed by one of the strangest conquests in history (page 28). Mysteriously, the city was abandoned even before it was completely finished. Miraculously, the Spaniard conquistadors never found it. Its superb engineering has withstood earthquakes, five centuries of neglect, and invasion by the tropical jungle. In July 1911, it was discovered almost accidentally by an American (page 30).

Although it is possible to visit Machu Picchu as a day-trip from Cusco (Qosqo*) by train or helicopter, hiking the trail provides the most authentic and satisfying approach. After walking for several days through spectacular valleys, visiting ruins that are successively finer and more extensive, the stage is set for your final approach to Intipunku, the 'gate of the sun'.

From Intipunku, the spectacle below of the ruined city draped over its ridge is so compelling that it must have been planned. The Incas surely created this succession of vistas culminating in Machu Picchu as both a pilgrimage and a religious work of art on a vast scale.

The trail makes imaginative use of sculptured staircases and bold tunnels. The Incas designed and built all their constructions to fit intimately with their natural surroundings. They were strongly committed to suiting each feature, every last stone, to the contours of the site. Gigantic stones were moved, carved and polished as a labour of love. Yet these great works were achieved by a civilisation with neither knowledge of iron nor benefit of the wheel.

It is impossible to hike the trail without being impressed and moved by the ingenuity and dedication of the Incas. And as visitors we benefit from the wisdom and stamina of the Andean guides and porters, direct descendants of the Incas and custodians of their heritage.

*For pronunciation and spelling of these and other words, please see the notes on page 61

Background: Inca stonework (see lower photograph on page 27)

Planning your trip

What is the best time of year?

The Inca trails covered by this book start with a journey from Cusco, the old Inca capital, to their various starting points and finish at the lost Inca city of Machu Picchu. Close to the equator (13° south), the sun is always nearly overhead, and at altitude the daily temperature range is extreme. The rainy season lasts from December to March, when visibility is poorer and conditions less pleasant, although plant life is lush and the trail less crowded. Avoid January and February anyway. Remember that rain, mist, snow and thunderstorms can occur at any time of year.

July and August are peak months for numbers and pressure on facilities. Ideally, aim for April to June or September to November for the Classic Trail. However, the Mollepata Trail is possible only from May to late September/early October because heavy snow makes the route dangerous or impassable outside that period (see pages 6–9). If you are interested in the winter solstice festival (Inti Raymi), re-enactments take place at Saqsaywaman (Cusco) and elsewhere, annually around 24 June; naturally these attract large crowds.

Other factors to consider include allowing time to learn some Spanish and/or Quechua (see page 61) before your trip, and time to prepare yourself physically for a tough hike reaching altitudes ranging from 2700 to 5000 metres (depending on the route: see page 7). Before booking your departure, read pages 9 to 16 to help decide how much preparation time you will need.

Choose your tour operator carefully. Recent regulations mean that you can no longer hike the Inca Trail independently. The simplest approach is to book in advance a complete package, with or without flights, using brochures and websites for guidance, see page 63. Beware of the budget operators, which often pay their porters very badly, use poor camping equipment and may expect you to carry everything except tents and cooking equipment. Check exactly what is included: some apparent bargains are less attractive when you find you have to buy your own entry, bus and train tickets on top of the 'package' figure.

View over Cusco, the ancient Inca capital

Combining it with other activities

For most visitors, the air fare to Peru is a significant sum. If you can spare an extra week or two, it makes sense to combine an Inca Trail holiday with other activities. You are almost certain to start from the ancient Inca capital of Cusco. It is at high altitude (3350 metres, 900 metres higher than Machu Picchu) so your body can begin to acclimatise while you meander around its sights or use it as a base for exploring the Sacred Valley. Further south and bordering Bolivia, Lake Titicaca is the highest navigable water on the planet, and a visit there can be combined with Cusco and hiking the Inca Trail.

Those with more time to spare could visit the Amazon jungle to the northeast, or travel northwest to Ecuador and the Galapagos islands. Given time and budget, you have the whole of south America to choose from. Whatever you do, plan to include a few days at high altitude before embarking on your hike.

The rainbow flag of Cusco flies in its main plaza beside the Peruvian flag

Which Inca Trail?

In its heyday, the Inca empire had a road network stretching thousands of miles from Colombia to Chile (see page 28), and there is good hiking among the Inca trails of Bolivia, for example. However, this book focuses on the most famous one, to Machu Picchu in Peru, by way of three contrasting routes which we call Classic, Mollepata and Shortest. Further variations are possible, but these three offer a wide range of choice and suit most people's needs.

The Classic Trail starts at or near Chilca from railway halts Km 77, 82 or 88, and normally takes three or four days. Some books describe this as 'the Inca Trail' as if no other existed, but two other choices are popular. For more of a wilderness experience, start from the village of Mollepata in the south, a tougher, more scenic route lasting five or six days. For those with no time to spare, the Shortest option starts from railway halt Km 104 and takes a single day to hike. (Incidentally, this is sometimes referred to as the *Sacred* or *Royal Trail*, but these adjectives are applied to other trails too.) To all of these estimated hiking times, add at least a full day to explore Machu Picchu itself (see pages 56-60).

Compared with any rambling that you do at home, the modest distances may lead you to underestimate the challenge. Even the Classic Trail (total length around 40 km) is fairly demanding because

- gradients are generally steep
- the altitude makes you short of breath
- the stones are unyielding to walk on, and
- the path is often narrow and sometimes edged by a steep drop-off.

Study the altitude profiles on page 8 and map (inside back cover) to see how the routes compare. The table below shows which sections in Part 3 describe each

The dramatic Chiriasca Pass on the Mollepata Trail, altitude 5000 metres

route. Standard yellow panels at the head of each section include an average hiking time: this figure relates to walking only, making no allowance for meal stops or for visiting ruins. Of course, your group may walk faster or slower than these times, but the differences will be broadly consistent. Such times provide more useful guidance than distances.

Trail	Duration of hike in days	Described in book sections	Map panels (back inner flap)	Highest altitude metres	feet
Shortest	1	3·1, 3·7	2	2700	8850
Classic	3 – 4	3·5 – 3·7	2 – 3	4200	13,800
Mollepata	5 – 6	all except 3·1, 3·5	1, 2 – 3	5000	16,400

Because of the variety of transport options, multiple starting-points and differences in pace, not all Part 3 sections correspond with a day's walk. For example, section 3.4 is only a half-day and 3.5 anything from a half-day to a full one, depending on the starting-point and departure time from Cusco.

The Mollepata Trail joins the Classic Trail at Wayllabamba, and section 3.6 covers all the way from there to Phuyupatamarka, even though the walking time and number of ruins makes this too long for a single day. In practice, most groups overnight at a campsite beyond Wayllabamba, reaching Runkuraqay or Phuyupatamarka the following day.

After visiting Machu Picchu, almost everyone returns to Cusco by train from Aguas Calientes, so this book does not describe the return journey.

Inca Trail altitude profiles

Figures in this diagram (and throughout the book) are based on the authors' GPS readings, suitably rounded to allow for the range of altitudes occupied by ruins and campsites, and for satellite error.

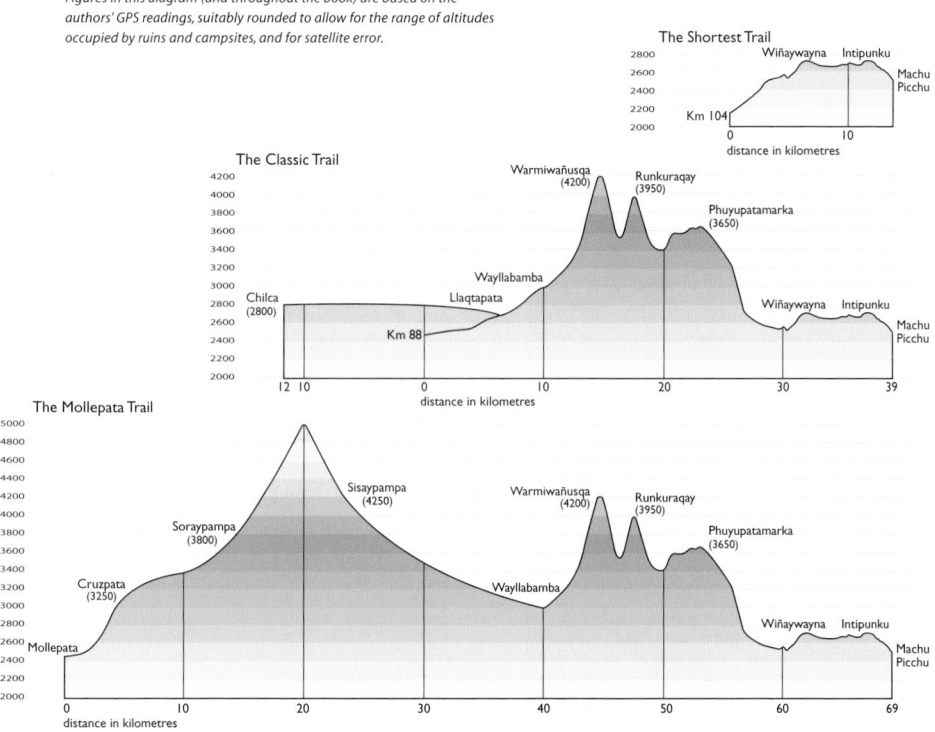

Your choice of trail will be influenced by how long you have to spare as well as how experienced and confident you are at hiking. The Mollepata route is more strenuous than the Classic, because

- you walk twice as far, and
- you climb higher (to 5000 metres on your second day) so you are at greater risk of altitude symptoms.

On the other hand, Mollepata takes you away from the crowds, around the shoulder of the beautiful mountain Salkantay (6271 metres) along a route with magnificent scenery. Because it joins the Classic route at Wayllabamba, arguably you get the best of both trails. If you are confident of your fitness and can take the time necessary to do it between May and September, it is the recommended choice.

On the Mollepata Trail

Finally, if pressure on your schedule dictates that you take the Shortest Trail, don't neglect your fitness or the altitude effects. You face a full day's hiking at altitudes of 2100 to 2700 metres, and if your body is unprepared, you may not enjoy Machu Picchu the next day. Exertion is a major risk factor in altitude sickness (pages 12-14), and some people experience symptoms even at this level, especially if unaccustomed to exercise.

Fitness, exercise and heart rate

Muscles get stronger if they are used regularly, at a suitable level and for a sustained period. This is known as the training effect. As a hiker, you might think the most important muscles to train are in your legs, but in fact the heart is even more vital. If you train your heart muscle, it pumps blood more efficiently and delivers more oxygen. Cardiovascular (CV) fitness refers to your heart and lungs: you will improve your CV fitness simply by exercising in your fitness target zone for at least 20 minutes several times a week.

Your target zone

This table shows how the target zone is calculated by age, though the formula does not allow for individual differences. Exercising above the target zone will not increase your CV fitness significantly further, and may tire you faster. Exercising below it will benefit you in weight loss, increasing your power-to-weight ratio, but it will not noticeably improve your fitness level.

If you exercise within the target zone for 20-40 minutes every other day, within a few weeks you will notice your fitness level rising. You will be having to work harder to push your heart rate into the target zone, and it will return to normal faster whenever you slow down. The guideline is to work hard enough to make you pant, but not so hard that you cannot also talk. A wrist-worn heart rate monitor takes out the guesswork by showing you a continuous read-out.

Age range (years)	Target zone (beats per minute)
16 – 20	140 – 170
21 – 25	136 – 166
26 – 30	133 – 162
31 – 35	130 – 157
36 – 40	126 – 153
41 – 45	122 – 149
46 – 50	119 – 144
51 – 55	116 – 140
56 – 60	112 – 136
61 – 65	108 – 132
66 – 70	105 – 128
71 – 75	102 – 123
76 – 80	98 – 119

How your target zone varies with your age

The fit person climbs more easily and uses less oxygen per unit of work done. When everything takes more effort than usual, as at altitude, it helps if your heart is pumping the available oxygen to your muscles and brain efficiently.

If you need to lose weight it makes sense to do so well before your trip, and gradually. Carrying surplus fat adds to your baggage and makes hiking more of an effort. However, don't go to extremes: fat insulates your body from cold, and if you are very thin, you will have to carry more clothing to avoid hypothermia, especially at night.

Where and how to exercise

The answer depends on your preference, your lifestyle and where you live. If you live in or near pleasant terrain for walking/jogging, have considerable self-discipline and don't mind the weather, suitable footwear may be all you need. Consider getting a heart rate monitor to make your training more systematic. Try going out with a friend who also wants to get fit: if your training needs and paces are compatible, you will motivate each other.

If brisk walking or jogging does not appeal, find a mix of activities that you enjoy and can do often enough (three times per week). If you dislike an activity, you won't stick to it. Anything that puts your heart rate into the target zone is fine, eg energetic dancing, cycling or swimming. Consider joining a gym or fitness centre, as their equipment is designed to measure and build CV fitness. A gym makes you independent of the weather and hours of daylight, there are trained staff, and it's easy to monitor your progress.

Avoid relying on a single form of exercise. The smooth flat surface of a treadmill does nothing to prepare your leg muscles for rough terrain or steep descents. If you use a gym for convenience, try to complement it with some hill-walking in the weeks prior to departure, preferably on consecutive days and with steep ascents and descents.

However you exercise, minimise the risk of straining your body, especially at first, by warming up slowly beforehand, cooling down afterwards, and stretching both before and after. Stretch beforehand to reduce the risk of injury, but make sure your muscles are warm before you stretch. Stretch after exercise to prevent a build-up of lactic acid in your muscles, which leads to stiffness the next day. Take a water container and drink plenty before, during and after your sessions.

When and how often to exercise

You don't have to become an exercise junkie to walk these trails, nor give up your normal pleasures, but if you become fit you will enjoy the experience more. Start training long before you go: if you are very unfit, aim to start three to six months in advance. If you smoke, give it up at least until after your trip.

For CV fitness, you need at least 20-minute sessions for maximum training effect, but build up to 30 minutes, and, approaching your departure date, 40-60 minutes. Better still, spend some time walking fast on rough or hilly terrain to prepare your body for sustained effort.

The best frequency for training is every other day: the body needs a rest day to extract maximum benefit from the training session. Since you may miss the odd session, three times per week is the goal for your main training period. Prior to departure, build up to longer sessions and higher target heart rates. Stop training a day or two before you leave, and plan your trip to stay the first two or three nights at higher altitude, taking minimal exercise on arrival.

Altitude effects

This section explains the cause of altitude problems and how to prevent or minimise them. We have tried to summarise the relevant bits of a large technical literature, using a minimum of medical jargon, focusing on practical advice and drawing also on experience gained at first hand. For more detail, please consult one of the many books or websites written by experts on high-altitude medicine (page 62).

How your body responds to lack of oxygen

The altitude problem for your body is the shortage of oxygen. As you climb higher, the air gets thinner. At 4200 metres (the highest point on the Classic Trail) atmospheric pressure is little over half its sea level value; at 5000 metres (the highest on Mollepata) it is lower still. Approaching these altitudes, each lungful gives you about half as much oxygen as at sea level, so your heart and lungs have to work twice as hard to maintain oxygen supply to your tissues.

Basically, your heart is the pump that makes your blood circulate. The lungs load the vital oxygen into your red blood cells for delivery to your tissues (muscles, brain and other organs). The demand from your muscles depends on their activity level, but your brain needs a surprising amount of oxygen (15% of the total). If your brain lacks oxygen, your judgement declines, movement control suffers and speech becomes confused.

Your body responds in various ways to needing more oxygen:

- you breathe faster and deeper
- your heart beats faster, increasing the oxygen circulating to your tissues and forcing blood into parts of your lungs which aren't normally used
- your body gets rid of excess fluid and creates more red blood cells, making the blood thicker.

The timescale of these responses varies: you start to breathe faster right away, and your heart rate rises within minutes. It can take several days before your blood starts to thicken: if you notice that you are urinating a lot, that is probably a sign that your body is acclimatising. Making more red blood cells is a much longer process, taking a week or two to get under way: on most schedules, this won't happen in time to make much difference.

At altitude, breathe deeply and freely as far as possible. Sleep is an important time for the body's adjustment. Avoid sleeping pills and alcohol, both of which depress breathing while asleep. Allow digestion time after your evening meal before going to sleep.

Be aware of some other effects of altitude. Some people (especially women) experience swollen hands, face and ankles, so remove any tight-fitting jewellery before going to altitude. Contact lens wearers may find that the lenses become painful to wear at altitude, and should take spectacles as an alternative. Many people find they make more intestinal gas at altitude, but this is harmless unless your companions lack a sense of humour.

Acute Mountain Sickness (AMS)

Acute Mountain Sickness is what medical people call altitude sickness. 'Acute' here means that the onset is sudden, not that you will be acutely ill. If mild or moderate, AMS symptoms may disappear if you rest and ascend no further; if they are severe, you must descend. If you ignore the symptoms and behave unwisely you might become seriously ill.

Individuals vary widely in how they respond to altitude. Factors such as age and gender affect your chances, although doctors cannot explain why. Females are less likely to experience AMS than males. At moderate altitude, young people are more likely to suffer AMS than their elders: the risk decreases with age in an almost straight line.

From an aeroplane window, Lima to Cusco flight

You need to recognise whether AMS is mild, moderate or severe. Mild AMS feels like a hangover and can affect people at any altitude above 2100 metres (7000 feet), occasionally even lower. Its commonest symptom is a headache (which should respond to aspirin, paracetamol or ibuprofen) combined with at least one of the following:

- feeling sick
- lack of appetite
- sleeplessness
- general malaise (feeling lousy, lacking energy).

Altitude has a dehydrating effect, and dehydration alone can cause headaches. So if you have a headache, first drink a litre of water, perhaps with a mild pain-killer. If the headache disappears and you have no other symptoms, your body was just reminding you to drink more fluid. Mild AMS is bearable, and if it goes away after a rest or a downhill stretch you will be able to continue walking.

Moderate AMS is seriously unpleasant, whereas severe AMS is dangerous and could even be fatal if you were rash enough to ignore the symptoms. Moderate AMS differs from mild in that:

- there is likely to be vomiting
- the headache does not respond to pain relief, and
- the victim may be very short of breath even when not exercising (eg after 15 minutes' rest).

Severe AMS can develop from moderate AMS if symptoms are ignored; it may involve ataxia (loss of muscular co-ordination and balance), altered mental states such as confusion, aggression or withdrawal, and serious complications followed, if untreated, by death.

Severe AMS or complications are *very unlikely* on the Inca Trail if you follow a sensible itinerary and react appropriately to any warning signs. Any symptoms that persist overnight should be taken seriously.

In summary, AMS is avoidable and treatable, very simply, as follows:

- if you have altitude symptoms, rest, drink fluids and do not ascend further until they disappear
- if you are getting worse, or have complications, descend at once.

Diamox, coca and other drugs

The medical research literature on drugs and altitude illness is extensive, and acetazolamide (trade name Diamox) has been studied for over 25 years. When you exert yourself at altitude, you pant, venting off a lot of carbon dioxide; this can reduce the acidity of your blood. Diamox blocks or slows the enzyme involved in converting carbon dioxide, thereby stopping the blood from becoming too alkaline and stimulating the rate and depth of breathing. As a result, it speeds up acclimatisation. Some people take Diamox with them because it can help to prevent, as well as treat, AMS.

In most countries, you need a doctor's prescription for Diamox. Before rushing off to get one, however, consider the possible downside. It has been known to cause severe allergic reactions in a few individuals. So you should try it out ahead of your trip to test if you are allergic, to experiment with dosage and to discover whether you can tolerate the side-effects. These include:

- increased flow of urine (diuresis)
- numbness or tingling in hands, feet and face
- nausea and/or bizarre dreams
- finding that carbonated drinks taste flat.

Since altitude has a diuretic effect anyway, many people prefer to avoid Diamox as it creates further interruptions to sleep in order to urinate. Some doctors say this is a problem of excess dosage. The recommended dosage used to be 250 mg three times a day, starting several days before ascending. Stephen Bezruchka (see page 62) suggests trying 125 mg daily at bedtime starting on the day before ascending, and increasing the dosage only if need be. Medical authorities tend to favour Diamox, especially for the minority who are unusually susceptible to altitude symptoms. However, most hikers don't need it, and a few who use it have symptoms regardless.

Coca leaves have been chewed in the Andes for thousands of years and are an important part of the indigenous culture. In Inca times, coca was reserved for those of noble birth, but the Spanish gave it to overworked labourers to suppress hunger and fatigue. Its anaesthetic effect may help to mask altitude symptoms such as headaches, but it doesn't affect the underlying physiology in the same way as Diamox. AMS is rare among residents because they are acclimatised, rather than because they chew coca leaves.

When people chew a quid of leaves together with a catalyst called llipta, a natural anaesthetic is released. This is not cocaine, a highly refined alkaloid, although coca leaves are the raw material from which this class A narcotic is made. You are unlikely to find coca-chewing addictive, and some people find it unpleasant. Try drinking maté de coca, tea made from coca leaves, which is also alleged to relieve altitude symptoms. It is widely available in Cusco, but don't take any home since in most countries coca leaf is a prohibited drug and its importation carries a prison sentence.

Finally, although coca leaves are legal and commonplace in Peru, do not assume that it is safe to buy or use other drugs: police informants are active, and drug use or possession carries a prison sentence of up to 15 years.

Advice on food and drink

Tour operators are responsible for food, fuel and cooking equipment, and their cooks produce plenty of palatable food despite difficult conditions for preparation and serving. Don't expect a choice of menu, and if you are vegetarian or vegan, discuss this beforehand. A diet rich in carbohydrates helps to prevent altitude symptoms.

Food is plentiful and rich in carbohydrates

Bring some snacks such as dried fruit, trail mix, cereal bars or chocolate. They will boost your energy and morale and can be shared with others. Bring also some sweets because many people suffer very dry throats at altitude.

Few people carry sufficient water, and even fewer keep it handy. You dehydrate quickly when walking at altitude: every time you breathe out, you lose moisture. Also altitude has a diuretic effect, and especially when exercising you are continually losing water vapour as invisible sweat. Expect to drink two to four litres per day on top of the liquid you take with meals.

Try to drink before you become thirsty. A water bottle or bladder with tube (eg a Platypus) is ideal as it lets you take sips whenever needed without having to stop or fiddle with rucksacks. (Disposable plastic water bottles are not allowed on the trail because of the litter problem, but refillable water bottles or bladders are fine.) If in doubt, check the colour of your urine: pale straw colour is healthy, but yellow warns that you are dehydrated.

Keep water purification drops or tablets handy and carefully follow the instructions about standing time and dosage in cold conditions. If the flavour bothers you, neutralise it with Vitamin C tablets or fruit-flavoured powder.

Help to limit fluid lost through sweating by adjusting your clothing. Try to anticipate your body's heat production. Shed excess layer(s) just before you start to overheat, and restore them just before you start to chill (eg for a rest stop or when the weather changes). Because each of these actions means stopping and fiddling with your rucksack, it may be easier to keep a steady pace and wear clothes designed for flexibility. For example, jackets should have underarm zippers and pockets large enough to hold gloves and hat.

At altitude, keep your water bottle or bladder well insulated or warmed by your body heat, otherwise it could freeze during the night. If you use a water bladder, the narrow tube is prone to freeze, so either keep it protected or else blow back the water left in the tube after each sip so that it remains empty.

Summary: how to prevent and manage AMS

- prepare well by becoming fitter (and giving up smoking if need be)
- plan your trip to start with a few easy days at high altitude, eg Cusco
- drink plenty of fluids (three to five litres per day), especially water
- avoid sleeping pills and alcohol
- eat small amounts of food often, even if you don't feel hungry; avoid excessive salt
- if you have altitude symptoms, rest and do not ascend further until and unless you have recovered completely.

Other health issues

Before you commit yourself, talk to your doctor (general practitioner or physician), taking the altitude profiles (page 8) with you. Unless your medical history includes serious risk factors, your doctor will probably be enthusiastic about the healthy side-effects of sound preparation.

Take this chance to check the latest information on which vaccinations against diseases are required and recommended for Peru, and what is the timetable. Ensure that you store your vaccination records safely. Take advice about anti-malarial drugs and insect repellents and follow it carefully. Malaria is a life-threatening disease which is easy to prevent but difficult to treat. Those who are spending time at lower altitudes in Peru will certainly need protection. Some people, especially on longer and more remote tours, wish to take a broad-spectrum antibiotic: if this applies to you, discuss it with your doctor.

Your feet are about to become the most important part of your body, so consider seeing a chiropodist and carry blister prevention and treatment. If you are a blood donor, make your last donation at least eight to ten weeks before you leave. Remember to visit your dentist well before departure.

Many tourists experience digestive upsets in Peru, mainly because their systems cannot cope with food and water that is contaminated by dirty water, dirty hands or flies. Some simple precautions can reduce the chances of diarrhoea, which is both uncomfortable and dehydrating. The standard advice for food is 'cook it, peel it, wash it, or forget it': this is sound, but not sufficient. Beware of dishes such as lasagne and quiche that have been cooked earlier in the day and then reheated; they are prone to contamination between being cooked and served.

Beware also of blended fruit and yoghurt drinks, undercooked meat, ice-cream products and ice, since freezing doesn't kill micro-organisms. Food that is thoroughly cooked and served immediately should be safe. Keeping yourself clean while camping isn't always easy, so take a good supply of wet wipes, preferably medicated, and be scrupulous about cleaning your hands before touching food or eating implements.

Drinking water must be boiled or purified chemically. At any altitude, boiling water even briefly makes it safe to drink. Filtration alone gives no protection against viruses, which can pass easily through the finest filter you can buy: they protect only against bacteria. Iodine drops (or tablets) are better than chlorine because they protect you against giardia. However, iodine is not suitable for pregnant women or those with thyroid conditions, nor for anybody to use long term. For trips of up to a month it is the preferred option. Anything destined for your mouth (toothbrush or food) needs to be washed in water that has been purified or boiled.

In case you are unlucky, despite these precautions, consider what anti-diarrhoea medicine to take. Bowel paralysers such as Imodium relieve the symptoms and will help to sustain your hike. Rehydration salts such as Dioralyte can help you to restore your fluid balance faster. Most bacterial and viral diarrhoea clears up within a few days, so relieve the symptoms and be sure to drink plenty of fluids. If problems persist, seek medical advice in Cusco.

Peruvian plumbing cannot normally cope with toilet paper so don't try to flush it away, even in good hotels. If this strikes you as unhygienic, consider the effects of a blocked toilet, and use the bin provided instead. Responsible tour operators provide toilet tents at each camp for hikers' use, and dig deep holes inside them, which are filled in later. If there is a bin bag for toilet paper use it, or else put the paper in the hole for burying along with the waste.

Finally, remember that the sun's rays are far stronger at altitude, because the thinner air filters out less of the harmful radiation. Since the equatorial sun is already much stronger than most tourists are used to, the risk of sunburn is doubly severe. Take a wide-brimmed hat and cream with a high Sun Protection Factor (at least SPF 25) for your face and lips. Use top-quality sunglasses to protect your eyes.

Equipment and packing

There is a packing list on page 22. Major items include a well broken-in pair of walking boots, a suitable day rucksack and kit bag, walking poles, and sleeping gear for the very cold nights at altitude. Long before you set off, try out anything you buy specially.

Special footbeds can make boots more comfortable

Boots

If your walking boots need to be replaced, do it well ahead of time. Take or buy suitable socks and consider buying a special footbed to replace the one supplied with the boot. They are expensive, but can make a boot feel more comfortable and reduce friction by locating your heel more securely. Buy them together with the boots if possible, in case they take you to a larger size. Remember also that your feet vary in volume and shape according to what you have just been doing. After a long hike carrying a heavy rucksack, your feet will spread and swell, and you need to allow for this when deciding which size to buy. A common mistake is to buy boots that are too short. This may lead to serious toe trouble, especially on the steep descents. Specialist fitters can fix almost any other boot problem.

Rucksack and kit bag

Your day rucksack should hold at least 30 litres so as to store plenty of water and spare clothing. If in doubt, err on the large side for easier retrieval and packing. Either buy a waterproof cover or liner, or use a bin (garbage) bag inside it. Check that the rucksack –

- is comfortable to wear (test it with a heavy load in the shop)
- has a chest strap as well as a waist strap
- is easy to put on and take off
- has side pockets for small items
- has loops and straps to store poles (see below).

Everything that isn't in your rucksack will be in your kit bag, which will be carried by a porter. A suitable kit bag must be large, soft and light, without a frame, wheels or dangling straps. Rucksacks and conventional suitcases are unsuitable: try to get something waterproof, such as a sailing bag, sports holdall or ex-army kit bag. It should be tough enough to withstand aeroplane baggage handling, or else it must be packed inside something that is.

Trial packing

Long before you depart, do a trial pack, using your kit bag to find out if you are within target weight (6 to 10 kg depending on the length of your trail). Refer to the list on page 22, but leave out your hiking boots, as you will either be wearing them or else carrying them in your rucksack. Pack in your hand baggage anything fragile (torches, sunglasses, camera) and any medicines you might need during the flight, as well as your passport, ticket, vaccination records and other valuables. Take extra care about packaging and organising: clear polythene zip-lock bags are great for keeping small stuff handy and visible, and cling-film keeps moisture off batteries and other delicate items.

You may be leaving surplus kit behind before you set off on the trail. This might include spare toiletries and clothes, aeroplane reading, personal hi-fi and anything you need for other parts of your holiday. If possible, have a lockable bag for this purpose. You may be allowed up to 20 kg on the international flight, but your trail kit should weigh under 6 to 10 kg.

Walking poles

Even if you don't normally use poles, consider trying or buying them before this trip. They improve your balance, save effort and reduce knee strain, especially on the steep descents. A pair is better for balance and efficiency, but some people prefer to keep one hand free. Telescopic poles can be stowed on your rucksack loops when not needed.

Although the Inca Trail regulations appear to forbid metal poles, if the tips are properly protected you will be allowed to use them. Hiking shops sell special rubber tips that fit snugly and protect the stones. Don't try to use the flimsy plastic packing tips that come with the poles and are unlikely to outlast a day. The alternative of buying wooden walking poles locally is not recommended as it leads to the destruction of so many trees and loss of habitat. Anyway, wooden poles cannot be stowed on a rucksack and are less flexible than the telescopic metal type.

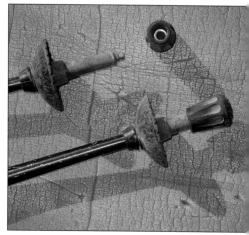

Poles need rubber tips for use on the Inca Trail

Warmth

Dress in layers to help control your body temperature. The base should be a 'wicking' fabric, such as knitted polyester. Over that wear a medium-weight fleece, then an outer layer which consists of waterproof jacket and trousers: choose 'breathable' waterproofs that allow sweat to evaporate. Take great care over good gloves, footwear and head/face protection, to avoid hypothermia.

Don't underestimate how cold you may be at nights, sleeping on cold ground at altitude. If you can't afford a really good sleeping-bag, borrow or hire one. A silk or thermal liner helps to keep a sleeping-bag warm, as well as clean. Most tour operators provide sleeping mats; if not, take with you a good self-inflating air bed. Cheap foam mats don't insulate well enough, and you can't enjoy your holiday if you are too cold to sleep. At higher altitudes, some people need to wear most of their clothes at night, including hat and gloves.

Packing checklist

The list below is divided into essential and desirable. Experienced hikers may disagree about what belongs in each category, but others may find the division helpful. You won't have access to your main kit bag all day, so carry everything you need for each day's walk: blister protection, water purification and medicines must be in your rucksack, not your kit bag.

Essential

- well broken-in walking boots
- plenty of good walking socks
- many layers of suitably warm clothing, including thermal underwear
- hat(s) and/or balaclava for wind and sun protection
- sun protection for eyes and face (sunglasses, high SPF suncream)
- gloves, glove liners and/or warm mittens
- waterproof jacket and trousers (breathable)
- water carrier(s) and water purification tablets or drops
- first aid kit, including blister, headache and diarrhoea relief
- toilet tissue (biodegradable)
- wet wipes and wash bag equipped for cleaning skin and teeth
- head-torch and/or pocket torch with spare batteries
- four- or five-season sleeping bag and (unless provided) sleeping mat
- enough cash in US dollars for tips for guides, cooks and porters, plus other holiday spending ; take plenty of small denomination notes. Travellers' cheques are valuable back-ups in emergencies.

Desirable

- pole(s) with rubber tips
- light and rugged camera; remember spare batteries and film
- waterproof rucksack cover or waterproof liner, eg bin (garbage) bag
- pouch or secure pockets: to keep small items handy but safe
- snacks and throat sweets
- thermal sleeping bag liner
- ear plugs (if you are a light sleeper)
- spare shoes (eg trainers or hut slippers), spare bootlaces
- paper and pen, playing cards or book
- guidebook and/or map.

2·1 Peru, tourism and conservation

Peru has become a much safer tourist destination than it was in the late 20th century, when political turbulence and hyper-inflation had given it a bad reputation. The terrorist campaign started in the 1980s by the Sendero Luminoso (Shining Path, a Maoist group) claimed some 30,000 lives and the country had come close to economic ruin.

Things improved during the 1990s, especially after the arrest of leading terrorists and economic reforms that brought down inflation. In April 2001, at his third attempt, Alejandro Toledo became Peru's first president of indigenous descent, helped by his Belgian-born wife who also campaigned in Quechua. Symbolically, Toledo was sworn in first in Lima, then at Machu Picchu, in July. Nowadays, tourists are made welcome in Peru, and if they behave appropriately, they are as safe as in any developing country.

Geography

Peru is over five times larger than Great Britain and the third largest country in South America, with a population of 27.5 million people. Working eastward from the Pacific Ocean, it can be divided into three zones:

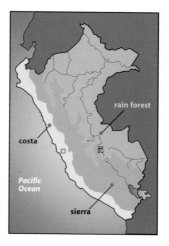

- the **costa** – the plain running along its 2500-kilometre Pacific coastline, where industry and commerce are concentrated; this contains the modern capital Lima, which alone has over eight million people

- the **sierra** or highlands of the Andes, covering 27% of the land area and home to about half the population; the climate ranges from temperate to very cold, with wide diurnal ranges and seasonally heavy rain; Cusco lies at altitude 3350 metres, whilst the Andes rise to over 6000 metres

- the **rain forest,** or Amazon jungle, covering 60% of Peru's area and home to less than 6% of its population; its hot, humid conditions support an incredible 10 million species of tropical flora and fauna.

Tourism and the economy

Although rich in natural resources such as minerals, fishing and agriculture, by western standards Peru is a poor country. The average Gross Domestic Product is only $4700 per head, compared with about $20,000 for the UK or $30,000 for the US. That comparison understates the poverty, because wealth is so unequally distributed. Some 70% of the population lives at or below the poverty level (1996 census), including a disproportionate number of the indigenous Andeans, who make up about half of the population.

Tourism earnings have become extremely important to the Peruvian economy. You are expected to barter both in the markets and also before getting into a taxi; but remember that driving a hard bargain is less important to you than to the Peruvian. At the end of your hike,

think of your tips as an important supplement to earnings for hard-working staff. In the unlikely event that service was not good, point out what was wrong and encourage them to put it right, but if they did well, be generous.

Reputable operators take pride in delivering high standards of service, and some develop long-term relationships with a particular village from which porters are recruited regularly. The energy, camaraderie and cheerfulness of the porters is a major ingredient in a happy expedition. Their speed and stamina while carrying heavy loads is legendary. When the new rules limited their loads to 25 kg, some complained that they could carry more: they were surprised to learn that on Kilimanjaro, the Tanzanian porters' loads are limited to 'only' 15 or 18 kg, depending on the route! Truly, the Andean porters are the chasquis (see page 28) of today.

The Inca Trail: conservation and regulation

The National Historical Sanctuary (map panel 1) is protected by law to conserve its biodiversity as well as the Inca ruins. Machu Picchu comes under intense pressure, with over 300,000 visitors each year. Daily from May to September, an average of 2000 people explore the ruins, of whom 150-200 have hiked the trail, perhaps 50 have come by helicopter and the rest by train.

Compared with many other tourist magnets, the Inca Trail is well maintained. The Peruvians have worked hard at limiting the erosion, litter and other damage caused by its popularity. This is a long-term campaign in which they need and deserve your support: choose an environmentally conscious operator and be careful about handling litter, where you go to the toilet, and

the use of poles. Happily, controversial plans to build a cable car and large hotel at Machu Picchu have been widely opposed, and the rules announced in 2000 (see panel below) were being enforced from 2001.

Since you are walking on ancient stones, the rule about protecting pole tips makes obvious sense (page 21). No disposable water bottles may be used, to reduce the litter problem. When visiting ruins, never climb on the stones or put your rucksack anywhere except on the ground. Although you may not see the rucksack rule displayed, local guides enforce it: as well as being a precaution against damage, it is a courtesy to other hikers.

Other rules prohibit acts of vandalism (such as picking wild flowers, camping in the ruins or making open fires) that no reader of this book would contemplate. Additional rules govern Machu Picchu itself: see page 55.

Inca Trail regulations (summary)

- All hikers must be accompanied by a licensed guide.
- Entry fee is $50 for the full trail or $25 for some shorter sections.
- Group size must not exceed 16 visitors.
- A maximum of 500 people per day will be allowed to embark on the Trail.
- Porters are not allowed to carry more than 25 kg.
- The trail will be closed for one month each year for maintenance (from February 2002).

2·2 The Inca civilisation: rise and fall

The Inca civilisation has left us a rich heritage: food such as potatoes, maize and quinoa; drugs such as quinine; and an amazing network of paved trails punctuated by superb ruins. Quechua, the official Inca language (see page 61), is still spoken by 10 million people to this day. Andean people maintain elements of the Inca religion, such as making offerings to apus, the spirits of sacred mountains, while also practising the Catholic religion. Above all, the Inca values of hard work and co-operation are obvious in the daily lives of their descendants.

The Incas and their predecessors developed fine arts to a high level, notably in textiles and weaving, ceramics and metalwork. They devised the 'lost wax' technique for making gold sculptures that is still used today by British dentists to shape gold fillings: during centrifuging, the heavier gold displaces the lighter wax. Sadly, the Spaniards melted down virtually all Inca gold and silver in an appalling display of greed and vandalism.

Inca architecture shows an almost religious commitment to suiting the design and choice of materials to the site. Time and again, you will see an interesting rock preserved in situ and skilfully worked into the structure. Inca stonemasons often expertly shaped huge rocks so as to echo and celebrate the silhouettes of sacred mountains. These are called 'image stones'.

Image stones representing the mountains Yanantin and Putucusi

Inca stonework is famous for its mortarless walls with large stones that fitted together with amazing precision. Not a blade of grass can grow in the gaps, yet the Incas had no knowledge of iron or steel and no machinery to move the stones. They worked with natural fracture lines in the rocks, sometimes drilling a line of holes which they plugged with wooden dowels; when dampened, these expanded and split the rock. Their shaping tools were made of bronze, silver and haematite, and they patiently sanded and polished the surfaces to finish them. Moving the huge stones into place needed great manpower. Although they used rollers of wood and stone, they never used wheels, perhaps because they had no metal strong enough to make an axle.

Pointer stone at Machu Picchu, aligned with the Southern Cross

Inca religion featured worship of the sun, moon and stars. Anyone who has felt the bone-chilling cold of a clear night in the Andes will understand why they revered the sun above all. They designed windows and markers to track and predict the winter solstice (page 59), and created pointer stones accurately aligned with sacred mountains or the compass points.

A young boy points out the puma's head in the pattern of stones in a Cusco wall

The Incas lived very close to nature. They worshipped mother earth, water and sacred crops including quinoa and coca leaves. Inca descendants still make offerings to Pachamama (mother earth). The three levels of the Andean world were symbolised by three animals: the serpent (wisdom and the underworld), the puma (power and the earth's surface) and the condor (the messenger of the skies). These levels are embodied in sacred stones with three steps.

Although we refer loosely to the Incas in general, at any one time there was only one Inca (the Sapa Inca), son of the sun, who acted as god, king and general combined. He ruled the empire through a sophisticated system of government, with taxes, controlled movement of population and a system of knotted cords, called quipus, for keeping records. At its zenith in the 15th century, the empire was over 5000 kilometres from north to south, and was covered by a vast network of fine roads. Fleet-footed messengers called chasquis ran barefoot in relays, bearing messages and goods. The Inca in Cusco could even enjoy fresh seafood brought 300 kilometres from the coast.

Red quinoa has nutritious, gluten-free seeds; cultivated since 3000 BC, it was held sacred by the Incas

Despite its high degree of organisation, the Inca empire was surprisingly short-lived. It was ended brutally in an infamous sequence of events. Francisco Pizarro, an illiterate Spanish peasant turned soldier, led a company of only 63 horsemen and some 100 infantry into the great Inca empire in 1532, seeking gold and other treasure. By a combination of shock tactics, treachery and lucky timing, this tiny force of conquistadors overcame the greatest empire of the day.

The Sapa Inca, Atahualpa, was told of the Spanish arrival by his chasquis. He was near Cajamarca with an army of thousands of fit, trained soldiers at the time. Surprisingly, despite being told of the Spanish raping and stealing, he agreed to meet them in the main square of Cajamarca. Atahualpa arrived dressed in great splendour but unarmed, borne high on a litter and followed by a procession of townspeople. The Spanish had set a trap, and when the signal was given their cavalry rushed out of their hiding places and butchered the natives, who were terrified by the new experience of horses and gunfire.

Atahualpa was captured alive; he offered to fill one room with gold and two more rooms with silver in exchange for his life. Misguidedly believing that the Spaniards would stick to the bargain, he told his leaderless army to disband. After the treasure had been brought from all corners of the empire by llama trains, the Spaniards treacherously murdered Atahualpa on 26 July 1533. He was sentenced to be burned at the stake, but after he converted to Christianity he was baptised and then garroted instead.

Inca resistance continued in various ways until the last Inca, Tupac Amaru, was captured in 1572 and executed in Cusco's Plaza de Armas. Meanwhile, the conquistadors had taken advantage of the confused succession: Atahualpa's half-brother Huascar had been defeated in a civil war only shortly before they arrived. They installed another of Huascar's brothers as a puppet Inca and received support not only from Huascar's faction but also from other native peoples who imagined that the Spanish would release them from Inca domination. What followed was centuries of exploitation and persecution, the destruction of monuments and the outlawing of their religion and even language.

To this day, the tension between the Hispanic colonial intrusions and the Inca legacy runs right through Peru. You see it in the dual systems of naming and spelling; you sense it in buildings like the Koricancha (Cusco) where crude Spanish bricks and mortar deface the older, finer Inca temple walls; and you hear it on the trail where the porters speak Quechua, but most guides speak Spanish or English to the tourists.

This account has only scratched the surface of Inca history and civilisation. Please see page 62 for suggested reading and recommended visits.

2·3 The mystery of Machu Picchu

Everything about Machu Picchu is surrounded by mystery. We don't know for sure why it was built nor why it was abandoned, and we don't even know its original Inca name. Machu Picchu is Quechua for 'old peak', the name of the mountain across whose shoulder the last part of the Trail runs.

The site consists of over 200 buildings, including residences, temples and utility buildings. These are connected by 109 staircases and flanked by many terraces which were mainly agricultural. Its population was probably around 1000-1200 people, and it may have been both a royal estate and a religious retreat, started in the mid-15th century under the Inca Pachacuti.

The buildings we see today are only part of the story: over 60% of the stones are underground, forming strong, earthquake-proof foundations. Machu Picchu is thus even bigger than it seems. Yet it is incomplete: there is evidence of work in progress, notably in

Machu Picchu's buildings feature many trapezoidal windows

the quarry and in the 'Temple of Three Windows' where a huge stone is poised as if still in transit. The site seems to have been abandoned unfinished after some 90 years, but there are no signs of violence, fire, epidemic or drought to explain why. Many theories have been published but none has been supported by convincing evidence.

Books often refer to the dramatic discovery of the 'lost city' on 24 July 1911 by Hiram Bingham. This is misleading: local farmers knew about the ruins all along. Indeed, two of them were peacefully farming terraces which they had cleared at the time of the 'discovery'. Bingham was an explorer whose expedition with friends from Yale University was mounted mainly to climb Mount Coropuna in the mistaken belief that it was the highest point in South America. He was also searching for Vilcabamba, the last refuge of the Incas founded by the Inca Manco who led the resistance to the Spanish after 1536. Bingham was not an archaeologist, and he describes in his memoirs (see page 62) how he had to consult the Royal Geographical Society's 'Hints for Travellers' for advice on what to do after discovering ruins.

On the historic day when he climbed up from his camp by the Urubamba, first with a soldier and then with an Andean boy as his guide, Bingham did not recognise the importance of his find. He spent only a few hours there, said little to his companions when he returned to their riverside camp, and did not even return next day. The scale of his discovery, which later made him very famous, did not emerge until his major expedition of 1912. His memoirs, written 35 years later, dramatise and compress these events; they also show that he still thought he had found Vilcabamba. The true Vilcabamba is at Espíritu Pampa, much deeper in the jungle, which Bingham also discovered.

Inevitably Bingham made mistakes in his interpretations, and nowadays many Peruvians are severely critical of him. Bingham's export licence for the antiquities he took back to Yale specified their return within nine months, but deplorably they remain in the US to this day. Bingham's book is full of admiration for Inca civilisation, and he devoted his life to studying and publicising Inca skills and techniques. Local guides might not have their jobs today had Bingham's team not persevered in their search and excavations. After all, Machu Picchu was so well hidden that the Spanish never found it.

Bingham's 'Temple of Three Windows' is a misnomer: the three-level stepped stone inside it suggests that this was a Temple of Pachamama

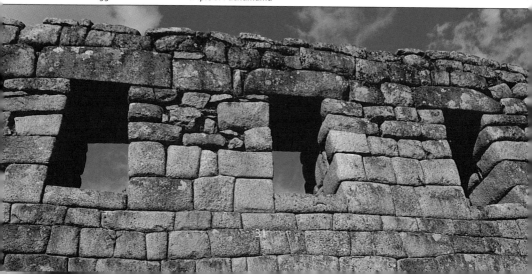

Vicuña are highly valued for their exquisitely soft wool

2·4 Andean wildlife

Peru has four camelid animals: two domesticated (llama and alpaca) and two wild (guanaco and vicuña). You will see many llama, which are widely used as beasts of burden. The one shown on page 33 is a Machu Picchu resident.

The rare vicuña is highly prized for its exquisite soft wool, the finest in the world. With a yield of only 250 grams per shearing, and only four or five shearings per lifetime, the animal is both endangered and protected. Vicuña wool was used exclusively for making the finest clothes for the Inca himself.

While hiking, especially near dawn or dusk, look out for viscacha, which resembles both rabbit and squirrel. The animal on the left was photographed by an observant hiker near the Warmiwañusqa pass.

A new rodent was discovered by an American researcher in 2000 while climbing in the mountains near Machu Picchu. She called this pale grey tree rat – as large as a domestic cat – *Cuscomys ashaninka*. Remains of similar rats had been found in tombs at Machu Picchu, but the tomb rats were previously thought to be extinct.

Viscacha live on rocky slopes

You are unlikely to see the rare, shy spectacled bear, sadly threatened with extinction. Each animal is largely black with a unique set of face markings in cream. Machu Picchu Sanctuary is one of only two conservation areas for the habitat of this endearing animal. They prefer to live in cloud forest at altitudes between 1900 and 2400 metres.

Bird life is extremely varied: over 370 species live within the Sanctuary. The largest is the condor, which feeds on carrion and weighs around 10 kg. Its body is black except for a white neck ruff. However, you are more likely to see condor at the Colca Canyon, near Arequipa, than on the Inca Trail.

Llama near the guardhouse at dawn, Machu Picchu

You will glimpse many kinds of hummingbird as they flash across the trail, especially during the approach to Machu Picchu where flowers proliferate. They scull their wings in a figure-of-eight at up to 80 beats per second while hovering to sip nectar or catch insects. For a close view, or a good photograph, you need patience and skill: and see page 43.

Other birds you may see include the mountain caracara, a scavenging kind of falcon; it occupies the niche filled by crows in temperate latitudes. On the higher ground you might see American falcon and buzzard eagle. Lower down, look out for the green streak of a passing parrot.

Peru's national bird is the Cock-of-the-rock. Males have dazzling bright orange heads and chests, and they gather twice daily in leks (groups) to make mating displays to the shy females. Its habitat is cloud forest up to 2400 metres. It may be seen in the ruins at Machu Picchu, mainly in the afternoons, and also along the Urubamba west of Aguas Calientes.

The Andean condor soars majestically with its 3-metre wingspan

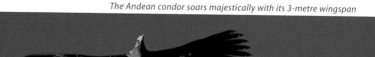

When near the Urubamba, look out for the amazing torrent duck, which uses its large muscular tail as a paddle to swim upstream in white-water rapids. The photograph above shows, from left to right, a male, a chick and a female.

In wooded areas and near water, look out especially for butterflies. Peru has more kinds of butterflies than any other country: over 3700 species, or one in five of the world's total.

The lower background photo shows mossy damp vegetation which thrives in the cloud forest. Inset at lower right is Teligpogon papilio, a rare orchid in danger of extinction.

Top: *Bomarea sanguinea* grows on other plants (altitude 3000+ metres)

Left: *Bromelia* at Machu Picchu

Right: *Sobralia dichotoma* (Paradise orchid) thrives in cloud forest

Background: Before Llulluchapampa, the Trail runs through a patch of polylepsis woodland, home to many rare birds

3·1 The Shortest Trail: from Km 104

Shortest

Time (average)	**4–6 hours (from Km 104 to Machu Picchu)**
Altitude gained	**600 metres (net)**
Terrain	**first section is a steady ascent on a good path; after Wiñaywayna the trail undulates, sometimes steeply**
Summary	**a useful route for those with very little time; not to be underestimated**

The Shortest Trail begins at Km 104, a halt on the railway from Cusco to Aguas Calientes. The train may not stop unless requested, and will not stop for long anyway, so watch the kilometre posts along the trackside. After you alight, look for the checkpoint to buy or show your trail ticket. Look down from the bridge over the river, keeping an eye open for torrent ducks (page 34).

Before you embark on this uphill hike across exposed terrain, make sure you have plenty of drinking water and good sun and wind protection. It will take two to three hours of steady climbing to reach Wiñaywayna, and a further two hours to reach the entrance booths of Machu Picchu. Most people do not visit the ruins until the following day.

The trail you are following was cleared and constructed only recently. It passes near an original Inca trail that climbs from the newly excavated ruins at Choquesuysuy, but is reserved for workers on the huge hydroelectric project.

Looking downstream along the River Urubamba (Vilcanota)

Looking across the steep terraces of Wiñaywayna to the trail traversing the hillside

Once across the river, the trail heads south-west past Chachabamba, with ruined buildings, a fine array of fountains or baths, a shrine and a round reservoir. It probably dates from the late 15th century, and had religious functions, perhaps also guarding access to Machu Picchu. It was uncovered by Paul Fejos' expedition in the 1940s, having been hidden by the jungle.

After Chachabamba, the trail heads south through woodland, then westward, beginning to climb seriously after it crosses a stream and passes under pylons. The ascent is never very steep, but there is hardly any shelter along the way and it can be very hot. The river is below on your right, and you will soon see glimpses of your first destination: first the tin roof of the modern hostel at Wiñaywayna, then the glorious terraced ruins themselves.

Wiñaywayna orchid

After a further climb, the path mercifully descends into the shady forest that surrounds Wiñaywayna. You reach a beautiful waterfall and soon emerge into the vertiginous terraces. The Wiñaywayna ruins are shown on page 53. You walk through the ruins and out past the hostel before joining the Classic Trail towards Machu Picchu: see page 54.

Wiñaywayna

Km 104

Machu Picchu

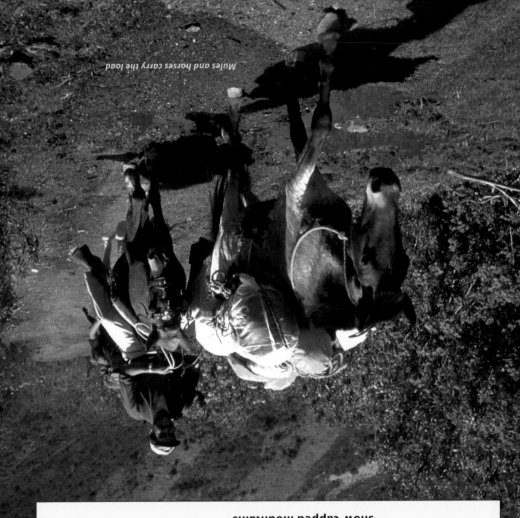

Mules and horses carry the load

3.2 The Mollepata Trail: to Soraypampa

Mollepata

Time (average)	4–8 hours (depending on starting-point)
Altitude gained	550 metres from Cruzpata, 1000 metres from Mollepata
Terrain	mainly good path, with some boggy sections and streams
Summary	a straightforward first stage, climbing steadily towards snow-capped mountains

Most people reach Mollepata after being driven for a couple of hours from Cusco along the spectacular, but sometimes tortuous, main road to Abancay; this provides splendid views of snow-capped mountains, including Salkantay and Waqaywillka (Verónica). After the Mollepata turn-out, you drive a further 40 minutes or so along a bone-shaking rough road to arrive at the main square of Mollepata village (population around 3000, altitude 2800 metres).

Some groups walk all the way from Mollepata, whereas others switch vehicles to ascend a very rough track by 4x4 trucks to a junction called Cruzpata (altitude 3250 metres). This option saves several hours of the less interesting part of this climb, and also allows you to cover more trail before camping, perhaps saving an overnight on this already long route.

The trail approaching Wamantay

Most operators use a mixture of mules and horses to carry camping gear and luggage along the first part of this trail.

Pack animals aren't allowed once you join the Classic Trail at Wayllabamba. It was hoof damage that destroyed the original Inca stones along the Classic Trail as far as Runkuraqay, so nowadays human porters carry the loads.

You climb steadily along the valley-side of the Rio Blanco, the river lying below you to your right. Soon you are walking towards your first snow-capped mountain: Wamantay or 'mountain of the falcons' (altitude 5917 metres). There is a campsite called Challacancha, but those who began from Cruzpata will keep on further up the valley. Shortly after the river cascades down a waterfall on your right, you reach the beautiful high campsite at Soraypampa (3800 metres), just below the tiny village of Soray.

Mollepata · Cruzpata · Soraypampa

3·3 Soraypampa to Sisaypampa

Time (average)	**6–8 hours**
Altitude gained	**1200 metres to the pass, 750 metres down to the campsite**
Terrain	**path variable, with some loose, steep sections, especially near the summit of the pass**
Summary	**a strenuous climb at altitude, rewarded by amazing views of Salkantay's glacier**

After Soray, you keep heading north-east up the valley, crossing and re-crossing the river, towards what appears to be a dead-end wall of scree. This is the terminal moraine (debris at the end) of Salkantay's glacier. To reach today's challenge, the highest pass of the whole trail, follow the path that climbs the right (eastern) side of the moraine. It is steep in places, and the gully gets narrower: just plod on steadily and you will make good progress.

Campsite at Sisaypampa, below Salkantay

Salkantay's majestic glacier, seen from the pass

The next campsite is called Pampa Japonés (altitude 4780 metres) after some Japanese climbers who attempted Salkantay unsuccessfully. Soon you can see the Chiriasca pass (see photo on page 7), up and to your right. This stiff climb will provide the most serious test of your fitness and acclimatisation so far. The path becomes very steep and the surface is very loose in places, but if it isn't misty or snowing you will enjoy fantastic views of Salkantay.

Pause at the top of the dramatic pass to enjoy views of the glacier and the valley beyond. You have already climbed higher than many mountaineers, and deserve a short rest before the steep descent. The glacier is the source of the River Kusichaca which will become your companion for the next section; it drains into the Amazon system, ultimately reaching the Atlantic.

The descent from the pass is very steep at first: take care not to slip. Poles are helpful, especially in the wet. After a while the gradient eases and the path meanders somewhat, generally heading north-east down the valley. Soon you reach the first beautiful campsite below: Sisaypampa (altitude 4250 metres).

Soraypampa

Sisaypampa

3·4 Sisaypampa to Wayllabamba

Mollepata

Time (average)	**3·5–4·5 hours**
Altitude lost	**1250 metres**
Terrain	**a steady descent on good paths towards the junction with the Classic Trail at Wayllabamba**
Summary	**mainly easy walking, with progressively lusher vegetation and more varied bird life as you descend**

From Sisaypampa, you follow the valley down, reaching a group of huts called Pampa Cahuana (3900 metres) within about an hour: this is a tiny place where another stream joins the Kusichaca from the south. Notice the remarkably straight section of river running off to the north-east ahead of and below you. This is the Inca canal: the Incas channelled the river to prevent it from meandering into precious farmland, and it performs that function to this day.

Just after a football field you cross the canal by a bridge. Observe the quality of the Inca stones that line it. After a while, both river and path swing northward, descending all the time. As it gets warmer, the sparse grasses give way to richly varied plants, supporting many more butterflies and birds.

The Inca canal

Salvia growing on a tree near Wayllabamba

Green violetear, one of 120 hummingbird species found in Peru

An hour and a half after the bridge, you reach your first Inca ruins: Paucarkancha lies at the junction of two rivers, commanding both valleys. It was a tambo, providing shelter and food for travellers, and also an important control point and communications post. The ruins date from the mid or late fifteenth century and have been reconstructed.

Two kilometres beyond Paucarkancha you reach Wayllabamba, strategically placed at the confluence of the rivers Llullucha and Kusichaca. These ruins were mainly agricultural, as the extensive terraces suggest. Shortly after, you reach the village, which is the last place to buy anything before Wiñaywayna, and you pass a campsite. You have now joined the Classic Trail.

The ruins at Wayllabamba command two valleys

Sisaypampa — Wayllabamba

3.5 The Classic Trail: to Wayllabamba

Time (average)	**2·5–5·5 hours (depending on starting-point)**
Altitude gained	**500 metres (from Km 88)**
Terrain	**mainly good paths and moderate gradients**
Summary	**a straightforward first stage, with rich plant life and some interesting ruins**

The Classic Trail usually begins at one of three train halts, generally known as Km 77, 82 or 88 (after their respective distances from Cusco by train). The village of Chilca (Km 77) is often reached instead by road, whereas Km 82 is used mainly, and Km 88 exclusively, by train passengers. The description below starts from Chilca, pointing out where other variants join the route.

Anyone travelling by train should be ready to jump out quickly; watch the kilometre posts along the trackside, or ask someone to warn you when you are near. As the railway runs north of the river and the trail on its south, you start by crossing a bridge, usually a short distance to the west of (ie beyond) the halt.

Bridge across the Urubamba rapids

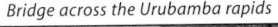

From the tiny village of Chilca (2800 metres), the walk begins gently westward, following a path along the south bank of the River Urubamba (Vilcanota). After a moderate descent, you pass through eucalyptus trees, and about half-way to Km 82 the trail swings north-west. Look out for interesting large cacti in this section. About 90 minutes after Chilca, note the bridge where walkers from Km 82 cross the river and turn right to join the trail (altitude 2600 metres). Look behind you from time to time, especially in clear weather, to see the snow-capped Waqaywillka (Verónica) towering over the flat valley floor.

'Prickly pear', a source of the dye cochineal

From Km 82 the trail runs south-west, at first climbing steeply away from the river. Soon it levels out, and you pass through a small village, shortly reaching Miskay where there is a control point for selling and inspecting trail tickets. Here the path runs south then immediately west, taking you down a deep gully and back up the other side.

Soon you reach the ruined hill fort of Willkaraqay, an ancient pre-Inca very small town, first inhabited around 500 BC. Its superb position commands the Kusichaca and Urubamba rivers, and it is said to have been the first site developed by the Incas after they arrived. From here, the view of Llaqtapata some distance below gives a clear idea of its layout (see page 46).

Next you travel a short way west and steeply downhill to meet the trail from Km 88 to Wayllabamba, turning left (southward) near the River Kusichaca, which flows into the Urubamba. Shortly you reach the campsite of Tunasmoqo, where those who began at Chilca may spend their first night.

Km 82

Km 77

Km 88

Wayllabamba

The ruins at Llaqtapata, with Pulpituyoc at far right

From Km 88 (or Qoriwayrachina), the trail differs at first. From the bridge, you start by walking back upstream along the Urubamba, then turn right up the Kusichaca. Soon you pass the important site of Llaqtapata, also known as Patallacta, first excavated by Bingham's team in 1915. Its fine terraces were used for growing maize and other crops, and it supplied food to Machu Picchu.

Llaqtapata was a major site, and its strategic position underlined the Inca presence and dominance. It housed a large number of inhabitants, including travellers and soldiers who manned the hill fort of Willkaraqay. It had religious and ceremonial functions, centred on the complex known as Pulpituyoc, the shrine with rounded walls visible at far right in the photograph below. It was probably built around 1450 and was abandoned 90 years later, after the Spanish invasion.

The River Kusichaca ('happy river')

46

After crossing the river, you climb up the hillside steeply, shortly to be joined from above by the trail from Km 82; you arrive at Tunasmoqo (altitude 2800 metres) just afterwards. From here on, the path is common from all starting-points, and it is only another five kilometres to Wayllabamba (altitude 3000 metres).

The path undulates but overall it climbs, whilst the valley narrows as you approach the bridge over the river. (Just before the bridge you can buy soft drinks from the trailside huts.) After a further half hour you cross the Llullucha river and arrive at the edge of Wayllabamba. The campsite here tends to be busy, and once it had a bad reputation for theft. Most groups press on for a few hours to another campsite (eg Llulluchapampa, at 3750 metres).

Opuntia Intermedia, another 'prickly pear'

The trail is rich in flowers and wildlife

3·6 Wayllabamba to Phuyupatamarka

Classic • Mollepata

Time (average)	**9–11 hours**
Altitude gained	**ascent of 1200 metres to the first pass, 450 to the second and 250 to the third, with a total descent of 1250 metres in between: overall net gain 600 metres**
Terrain	**Inca road and staircases give firm footing over some serious gradients**
Summary	**a demanding stage of switchback uphill and downhill, punctuated by increasingly fine ruins**

Porters approaching the Warmiwañusqa pass

From Wayllabamba to Machu Picchu, the route is common to the Mollepata and the Classic Trails (from any starting-point) and is described below. This stage is full of interest and challenge, punctuated by three passes and many ruins. It culminates in perhaps the most beautiful campsite of the whole trail: Phuyupatamarka. The photograph on the title page was taken from there.

The first pass is the highest on the Classic Trail, reaching an altitude of 4200 metres. This is a stiff climb, albeit 800 metres lower than the Chiriasca Pass (see page 7). The second pass is slightly lower at 3950 metres, and the third is lower again (3650 metres), and is approached by gentler gradients. However, late in the day, after many ruins, and steep ascents and descents, this can still be tiring.

Taking it step by step, from Wayllabamba the trail begins to climb steeply, often using flights of steps, through a narrow valley enclosed by dramatic mountains. It crosses a river

After the Warmiwañusqa pass, looking into the valley beyond

and passes through a lovely enclave of cloud forest (polylepsis, see page 35). Although you climb a large number of steps, you are not yet walking on original Inca stones, because they were destroyed long ago by mules' hooves: this section of trail was reconstructed in the 1990s.

After two to three hours' hard climb, you reach the Llulluchapampa campsite. This commands splendid views and has running water and a toilet block. If you look up and to the north-west, you can almost see the first pass, called

Wayllabamba

Phuyupatamarka

Warmiwañusqa or 'dead woman's pass'. There is nothing sinister about the name: it reflects the villagers' perception that the mountain shape resembles a supine woman. The top you see from here is actually a false summit, but the real one isn't much further.

From the campsite to the true summit is a steep climb of some 450 metres, spread over less than two kilometres of trail. If you have overnighted at Llulluchapampa, you will tackle this in the cool of the morning, when you are fresh. Take it slowly and steadily, and allow 1.5 to 2 hours, pausing at the top to enjoy the wonderful views. The next stage is a steep descent to Paqaymayo campsite, a drop of 600 metres over the next two kilometres.

After Paqaymayo, it takes less than a kilometre of steep climbing to the egg-shaped structure at Runkuraqay (3750 metres). These attractive ruins were heavily restored in the late 1990s. The site's main function was as a tambo,

Sayaqmarka ruins

where chasquis and others rested overnight. The circular area was a watch-tower, monitoring the two important routes that join here.

Not far above the ruins lies the second pass, at 3950 metres. First you reach a couple of false summits, but once you see the small lakes, you are near the true summit. You descend steeply at first, then more gently, enjoying fine views (weather permitting). Soon you will see the next ruins, Sayaqmarka (3600 metres), built on a dramatic rocky spur and commanding the trail beneath it. The path descends steeply, but to reach the ruins you climb a narrow, daunting staircase off to the left.

Runkuraqay ruins

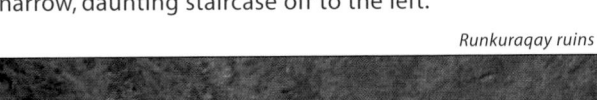

The ruins of Sayaqmarka are extensive, and over 50% original. It was the 1940s expedition led by Paul Fejos that gave it its name, which means 'inaccessible town'. Defended on three sides by its precipitous situation, it was a signalling point that overlooked the junction between the Inca trail to Machu Picchu and another old trail that follows the valley westward, down to the River Aobamba. The ruins probably date from the late fifteenth century. Slightly further on, near a stream, lies the tambo of Conchamarka, with small terraces for agriculture; Sayaqmarka has no terraces.

From Sayaqmarka to Phuyupatamarka (3600 metres) is a glorious section through high forest, with viewpoints over increasingly dramatic mountains and drop-offs. The path undulates,

View from the approach to Phuyupatamarka pass

sometimes steeply, and the stones you are walking on are mainly original. You descend through a superb long Inca tunnel before climbing towards the third pass along a magnificent ridge. Just before you arrive there, look out for a viewpoint over two river valleys, the Urubamba and the Aobamba. The campsite is just beyond the pass, and the ruins slightly below (see page 52).

Sayaqmarka has gracefully curved walls and a commanding view

3·7 Phuyupatamarka to Machu Picchu

Classic • Mollepata • Shortest

Time (average)	**5–6 hours**
Altitude lost	**1100 metres**
Terrain	**Inca road with steep staircases**
Summary	**a day of steep descent, culminating in your first glimpse of Machu Picchu, from Intipunku**

After camping, most people visit Phuyupatamarka's ruins the next morning. The design demonstrates the Inca passion for closely fitting the built environment to the natural contours of the site. Sinuous curves and serpentine terraces may suggest Gaudi's 20th-century architecture in Barcelona more than late 15th-century Peru. Although Bingham discovered this site, he left most of it still covered by jungle. In the 1940s the Fejos team uncovered the rest and gave the site its name: 'cloudy place'.

The five fountains were used for religious rituals as well as domestic purposes. There is an altar for llama sacrifice. The Incas worshipped water as the symbol of life, and Phuyupatamarka probably had key religious and ceremonial functions, especially for travellers on their way to Machu Picchu.

Phuyupatamarka ruins, with Machu Picchu mountain at upper centre and Intipata to its left

After the ruins, the trail heads downhill as an irregular staircase that drops 500 metres of altitude in 1300-1500 steps (estimates of the exact number differ). As you descend, the forest becomes denser, the vegetation more lush and the butterflies and birds more plentiful.

After 2-3 hours, you will reach a large pylon which marks a choice point. Ahead you will be able to see Intipata ('sunny place') – an extensive set of agricultural terraces that follow the convex contours of their spur. The site grew food (potatoes, maize, fruit and sweet potato) for Machu Picchu. Keep straight on to visit Intipata, and return afterwards to this pylon.

To continue the trail, turn right at the pylon and follow the steep downhill path towards the buildings of Wiñaywayna. The campsite here is always busy because it is the last one before Machu Picchu. There is a restaurant, hostel, proper toilets and a museum of a sort (stuffed animals). Once refreshed, take a ten-minute walk towards the beautiful ruins of Wiñaywayna (2650 metres), overlooking the Urubamba gorge. The terraces cling to the precipitous hillside with waterfalls beyond. 'Wiñaywayna' means 'forever young', and is the name of a pink orchid found around the site (see page 37).

Wiñaywayna ruins

Phuyupatamarka   Wiñaywayna   Machu Picchu

Like nearby Intipata, this site was agricultural, but Wiñaywayna was clearly more important. It has more buildings, finer stonework and a long flight of fountains, probably used in water ritual and worship. No irrigation was needed here, because of the rain-forest climate. Wiñaywayna is the last set of ruins before you reach Intipunku, and marks where the Shortest Trail joins the Classic and Mollepata Trails.

To continue towards Machu Picchu, return to the hostel and follow the trail for up to two hours (six kilometres). You are at about the same altitude as Intipunku but the trail undulates steeply in places. A flight of about 20 very steep steps announces that you are nearly there. After rounding a corner and climbing some gentler steps you reach Intipunku, the 'gate of the sun' (see arrow in the photograph below). From here, you look down on the awesome mystery of Machu Picchu, clinging to its steep hillside.

After this it is downhill all the way, with your destination in clear view. The path winds around the shoulder of Machu Picchu mountain, finally reaching the entrance booths and the exclusive Sanctuary Hotel, restaurant and outdoor café. From here you will either visit the ruins, or, if overnighting in Aguas Calientes, catch the bus down the hairpins of the Hiram Bingham road.

Aim for an early start next day: in late 2001, the first bus left Aguas Calientes at 0630. Early morning is cooler, clouds and mist are less likely, and you will avoid the crowds who arrive later by train.

The Inca Trail descends to Machu Picchu ruins from Intipunku (see arrow)

3·8 The destination: Machu Picchu

How you spend your time at Machu Picchu depends on your preferences, itinerary and travel arrangements. First some practicalities. If you are carrying a large rucksack and/or walking poles, you will have to check them near the entrance (small day-sacks are allowed). Once you pass the entrance booths, store your ticket safely for readmission later. Inside the site, there are no toilets or refreshments.

Wayna Picchu has terraces and ruins near its summit

Aim to visit as early as possible: in late 2001, the site opened at 0600 and became very busy between 1000 and 1500. Clouds tend to roll in during the afternoon, and early morning usually offers the best conditions. A return visit would be ideal, as there is so much to take in. If there is a full moon, consider an evening visit.

If your schedule allows a side-trip, you have a choice (see page 60). Try to plan your day to complete any strenuous walking early on, reducing bottlenecks on the steep narrow paths. The main site has around 3000 steps, and there is no shelter, so you will need water and sturdy shoes, especially for Wayna Picchu.

Start by climbing the path that leads up to the left, shortly after the entrance booths, to reach the guardhouse with the funerary rock. From here (altitude 2500 metres) you have a panoramic overview of the whole site. From the far end of the terraces, a path leads down to the ancient Inca entrance, taking you almost directly to the Sacred Plaza and on up to the Intiwatana group.

Overview of the site

To understand the layout of Machu Picchu, study the site plan (back cover outer) together with two bird's eye photographs: the front cover looks north toward Wayna Picchu from the guardhouse, and the photo on page 56 was taken from near the summit of Wayna Picchu looking back, southward.

Looking south over Machu Picchu from Wayna Picchu

Note the Inca Trail coming in from the top left corner, flanked by the upper and lower agricultural sectors. The roofed guardhouse is visible at upper left, perched above steep terraces, with cliffs and the Inca drawbridge down to the right. The Intiwatana pyramid is prominent at lower right, with the central plaza to its left. Between two roofed buildings near the bottom right there is a huge sacred rock: seven metres along its base plinth by three metres high. Some say it echoes the shape of the mountain Yanantin seen behind it, others say that it resembles Pumasillo in the opposite direction. Others again say the rock looks like a guinea pig or puma.

Massive sacred rock: mountain, guinea pig or puma?

The Sacred Plaza and Intiwatana group

The photgraph opposite looks northward across the Sacred Plaza to the Intiwatana pyramid. The small mountain behind is Uña Picchu (baby peak), not Wayna Picchu which is much taller.

The three-sided building (shown below the Intiwatana pyramid, and also in the photograph below) is the Principal Temple. Note how its beautiful stonework forms seven trapezoidal niches on its central wall, with five lower ones on each side wall. The gaps visible on the right are a result of settlement in Inca times, a rare by-product of imperfect foundations. Nevertheless, the stones fit so snugly that the building has survived half a millennium and many earthquakes.

The Intiwatana pyramid

The Principal Temple

The Intihuatana has an abstract mountain shape

Intihuatana means 'hitching post of the sun', a name applied by Bingham. It was not a sun dial, but related to the solar new year. Annually, just after the winter solstice, the Incas celebrated the Inti Raymi festival, with rituals to prevent the sun from slipping lower in the sky. The Inti Raymi was outlawed by the Spanish in 1572, but is re-enacted annually (see page 5).

The Intihuatana may have been linked with mountain worship, and its shape can be seen as an abstract image of a mountain. Its importance was shown by its position at the top of a huge natural pyramid reached by an imposing stone staircase, and was further emphasised by its huge rock base. Ironically and sadly, having survived undamaged for centuries, the Intihuatana was the victim of a careless crane operation during the filming of a beer commercial in September 2000. Look closely to see the chip near its top and the diagonal crack which runs across the stone.

The Intihuatana

The Temple of the Sun

The adjoining photograph looks north over the group containing the Temple of the Sun, or Torreon, with the Royal Residence, apartments for the visiting Inca ruler, beyond the thatched building. The Torreon's curved tower and superb stonework underline the importance of this temple.

The photograph below shows the most important window in the Torreon. At sunrise on the solstice (June 21), the shaft of light through this window aligns perfectly with a slot which the Incas cut into the rock. The red arrow below points to this slot.

The Temple of the Sun is at lower right

After visiting the Torreon, descend the stairs to find the cave below, deep in the immense rock formation on which the temple is built. Bingham called this the 'Royal Tomb'. Notice its superb stone stairways and the incredible hour-glass shape filling the three-dimensional jigsaw created between natural rock and Inca steps.

Machu Picchu is full of the genius of the Inca stonemasons, but this brief introduction is all that space allows. A good local guide will enhance your visit greatly; and see page 62 for a recommended guide book.

Alignment slot for observing the winter solstice

59

Wayna Picchu and other side-trips

The ascent of Wayna Picchu offers amazing views in all directions: the photos on pages 54 and 56 were taken from its summit. Before you begin, sign in at the caretaker's hut. In 2001, this trail was open only from 0700 to 1300, with bottled water on sale: but check in advance. Allow an hour to reach the very top, and three-quarters for the steep descent.

> ⚠️ The trail is very steep in places, and if the weather is or could become wet, be prepared to abandon it.
>
> The rock scramble can get very slippery, and a fall has proved fatal. If you suffer from vertigo, you should avoid this climb.
>
> In dry conditions, however, anyone of normal mobility can manage it. Take plenty of water and wear stout footwear.

The small tunnel before the summit

Follow the signs uphill, taking care on exposed sections. There are wonderful views on the way up, but the best panoramas are yet to come. Where the trail splits, keep right to reach a viewing platform with breath-taking 360° views. If conditions are not ideal, consider turning back; alternatively, climb up to and squeeze through the small granite tunnel, emerging to scramble over a jumble of huge boulders. These include a fine granite 'arrow stone' pointing at Salkantay, 20 km away.

Escape the summit area over the huge slide rock and descend past the restored observatory. Pause to reflect on the effort that went into creating and maintaining the terraces, tunnel and buildings in this precarious place.

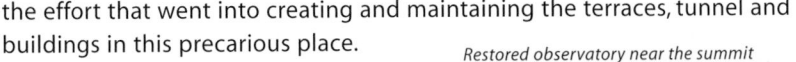

Restored observatory near the summit

Another side-trip is the 'Temple of the Moon': use the same entry-point but fork left at the sign after 10 minutes. It has superb stonework, but its trail is also very steep, with ladders, and it takes about two hours. There is also a short trail to the Inca drawbridge from the Guardhouse near the entrance. This is an easy 20-minute walk, but there are steep drop-offs: observe the warning sign. The fragile drawbridge underlines the utter remoteness of this hidden city, high in the Andes.

Reference

Quechua language and names

About ten million people, mainly living in the high Andes, speak Quechua, the largest remaining indigenous language in the Americas. It was the language of the Inca empire, and was outlawed by the Spanish regime in 1780. It survived centuries of persecution, and was granted official status only in the 1970s. However, Quechua is barely taught in schools and its position is undermined by Spanish.

Most English-language publications use Hispanic names and spellings throughout. In view of the Spanish record of destroying Inca culture, we feel that Hispanic spellings are deeply inappropriate for Inca ruins, and accept the difficulties that this brings. The Incas had no alphabetic system, and from the late 16th century both Spaniards and Incas used the Roman alphabet when writing Quechua. There are also regional variations in the language. You will often see several Quechua spellings of the same place name, even within the same document.

Many apparent inconsistencies disappear when you realise that 'hu' and 'w' are interchangeable, as are 'q', 'k' and 'c', and that place names may be shown as one word or two. Thus, for example, Huiñay Huayna and Wiñaywayna are the same.

Despite preferring Quechua spellings for ruins, we have retained Hispanic spelling for Cusco (rather than Qosq'o, Qosco or Cuzco), and for animals such as vicuña, to conform with local signage and reference sources.

Pronunciation

The spelling of many Quechua words suggests how they sound, at least approximately. However, we list here some common names that sometimes cause doubt or difficulty. Place the stress on the penultimate syllable. Correctly spoken, Quechua has many glottal stops and plosives, shown by apostrophes, but they are difficult for westerners to imitate, and for simplicity we have omitted them. Note the following pronunciations: the hyphens are for clarity, and do not suggest pauses.

Llaqtapata	yakta-pahta
Machu Picchu	machoo peechoo
Mollepata	moll-yeh-pahta
Phuyupatamarka	poo-yoo-patta-marka
Quechua	kech-wah
quinoa	keen-wah
Salkantay	sal-kant-eye
Saqsaywaman	saks-eye-wah-man
Wamantay	wah-mant-eye
Warmiwañusqa	wahr-me-wan-yus-ka
Wayllabamba	way-lee-ya-bamba
Wiñaywayna	win-yay-way-na

Some basic vocabulary

English	Quechua	Spanish
please	allichu	por favor
thank you	yusulpayki	gracias
you're welcome	imamanta	de nada
I'm sorry	dispinsayuway	lo siento
yes	arí	sí
no	manan	no
what?	ima?	qué?
where?	maypin?	dónde?
when?	hayk'aq?	cuándo?
how much?	hayk'an?	cuánto es?
bill	kwenta	la cuenta
let's go	haku	vamos
far	karu	lejos
near	sirka	cerca
difficult	sasa	difícil
easy	phasil	fácil
snow-capped	orqo	nevado
altitude sickness	suruchi	soroche

Recommended visits

In Lima, visit the gold museum (Museo de Oro del Peru). Despite its high proportion of fakes (over 80%), this collection gives insight into pre-Inca cultures. The Museo Rafael Larco holds the most amazing collection of 55,000 ceramic pieces, including superb Moche pots with thousands of human faces.

In Cusco, visit the immense ruins at Saqsaywaman. Built as an act of worship by a workforce of 20,000 men, it forms the head of the puma on which Cusco's design is based, its zig-zag walls being the puma's teeth. Despite its military role in the siege of Cusco and later use as a quarry by the Spaniards, the ruins remain impressive, with massive stones of over 300 tonnes.

Cusco's Inca museum gives good insights into Inca agriculture, medicine and fine arts. Don't miss the Centre for Traditional Textiles of Cusco, a living museum based within its courtyard. This imaginative project supports 2000-year old weaving techniques. You can watch the weavers in action and even buy an item from the person who created it. Visit their website in advance if possible: **www.incas.org**.

The Spaniards built the Church of Santo Domingo in Cusco on top of the superb mortarless walls of the Inca temple of Koricancha, and stripped from its walls 700 gold sheets of two kilograms each.

Further reading

1 Inca civilisation

The Incas: Empire of Blood and Gold Carmen Bernand, Thames & Hudson 1994 0-500-30402 Richly illustrated, thorough and compact, this covers social aspects such as the system of shared labour, taxes, family groupings, human sacrifice and mummification.

Lost City of the Incas Hiram Bingham, Condor Books/Special Book Services 2nd ed 1997

Bingham's own account of his discoveries, coloured by hindsight but very readable.

Ancient Kingdoms Nigel Davies, Penguin 1997 0-14-023381-4 Readable account of both pre-Inca and Inca civilisations, showing how our perceptions have been filtered by the Spanish chroniclers.

2 The Inca Trail and Machu Picchu

The Machu Picchu Guidebook: a self-guided tour Ruth M Wright and Alfredo Zegarra, Johnson Books 2001 1-55566-307-9 Detailed and up-to-date guide to the ruins, with many photographs and 162 pages of authoritative text; recommended.

Machu Picchu Historical Sanctuary Peter Frost and Jim Bartle, Nuevas Imágenes, Lima 1995 9972-9015-00-5 Has good photographs, with a chapter each on orchids and birds; 64 large-format pages

The Inca Trail: Cuzco & Machu Picchu Richard Danbury, Trailblazer 1999 1-873756-29-1 First edition was a thorough, reliable guide to the trails, with useful information on Lima and Cusco; very suitable for independent hikers (who are, alas, no longer permitted).

3 Languages and altitude illness

Colloquial Spanish of Latin America Rodriguez-Saona, Routledge ISBN 0-415-08954-9 (book and two 60-minute cassettes).

Quechua Phrasebook Ronald Wright, Lonely Planet 1989 0-86442-039-0 Pocket-sized and cheap, with a few oddities.

Altitude Illness: Prevention and Treatment Stephen Bezruchka, Cordee 1994 1-871890-57-8 Compact 93-page coverage of the causes, symptoms and signs, with decision trees, tables and interesting case studies.

4 Fiction

Into the Fire Linda Davies HarperCollins 2000 0-00-651188-0 Fast-paced thriller whose action heroine travels from the trading floor of the City of London to Peru; the plot culminates at Machu Picchu: engrossing aeroplane reading, with insights on Peru.

EXPLORE worldwide

Explore Worldwide Ltd has been operating tours and treks to Peru for over 20 years and offers all three Inca Trails described in this book. Explore also offers trekking trips around Huaraz and an exploration of the little-visited northern part of Peru. Three relevant tours are: –

Heights of Machu Picchu 15 days, includes the Classic Trail
High Trail of the Incas 14 days, includes the Mollepata Trail
Machu Picchu & Titicaca 19 days, includes the Shortest Trail.

Explore's tours offer the following benefits:

• conform to current trail regulations
• escorted by an Explore tour-leader and a Peruvian trekking guide
• overnight in the Machu Picchu area, allowing sufficient time to explore the site
• whilst on the trail, camping is fully supported: local staff erect tents, cook meals and carry your main pack; all you carry is your day-pack
• mess-tent, stools and therm-a-rests provided
• 20 years experience and reliable local partners.

Explore Worldwide Ltd
1 Frederick Street
Aldershot, Hants
GU11 1LQ

Tel: +44 (0) 1252 760 000 (reservations)
Tel: +44 (0) 1252 760 100 (brochure request)

email: res@exploreworldwide.com
website: **www.exploreworldwide.com**

Recommended website
www.ex.ac.uk/~RDavies/inca
Perhaps the most thorough and best maintained site on the worldwide web for the Inca Trail. It has an extensive Links page that gives access to the best of the rest.

Rucksack Readers
Uniform with this title, each Rucksack Reader features a world-class walk that can be completed inside a week. Three are low-altitude walks in Scotland: *The West Highland Way*, *The Great Glen Way* and *The Speyside Way*.

Explore Mount Kilimanjaro takes you from tropical rain forest to summit glaciers on the roof of Africa. At 5895 metres, for many walkers this is the highest point of their lives.

For information and online orders, visit
www.rucsacs.com
email: info@rucsacs.com
telephone (UK): 01786 824 696
outside UK: +44 1786 824 696.

Acknowledgements
The publisher wishes to thank the following for valuable comments on drafts: Dr Carol Darwin, MB, B Chir, Dr Maggie Eisner, Jo Field, John Telfer, Sir Robert Megarry, John Etchells, Les Smith and Brian Wall. Any flaws that may remain are our responsibility. Jacquetta also expresses heartfelt thanks to Fredy Medina and the Condor Travel team that supported her trek covering all three trails (September 19-26, 2001), specifically to research and take photographs for this book.

Photo credits
Roy Davies (p 46 lower), Michael and Patricia Fogden (p 43 upper), Fredy Medina Guzmán (p 40, p 41), Lindsay Merriman (p 32 lower), Tony Morrison/South American Pictures (p 28, p 32 upper, p 34 upper). Five images © Explore Worldwide slide library: p 24 upper, p 33 lower and p 37 lower (all James Sparshatt), p 7 (John Rutter), p 16. All other photographs © Jacquetta Megarry 2001.

Index